I

Didn't

HEAR

My Baby

CRYING

DR. APOSTLE ROBBIE CARSWELL

UNFAZED PUBLISHING
YOUR MIND IS OUR BUSINESS

TAMPA FLORIDA

DR. APOSTLE ROBBIE CARSWELL

ISBN: 978-1-959275-38-1

LIBRARY OF CONGRESS NUMBER: 2025942021

YOUR MIND IS OUR BUSINESS

UP UNFAZED PUBLISHING
YOUR MIND IS OUR BUSINESS

PRECISION IN AUTHOR THOUGHT

-INTRODUCTION-

I want to thank God for the grace to write my book. This book is not based on anything that is new. It is about things we dare not talk about openly in our lives. I shared with my family members that I was writing my book. When I told them what it would entail, I received many different attitudes from them. I really didn't stop or allow their opinions to hinder my decision. I think many will be amazed, as well as blessed, to read about this subject of violation in the family. I know this is common in society, but who have heard a woman of God that had to endure such a thing? I will expose the challenges in life as a woman of faith and how the Lord brought me through it. I have grown from the moment I acknowledged the act of molestation in my

Christian home. I never thought in my mind that I would have to suffer the pain of seeing my own child go through this vicious act. I walked through many questions once the issue was exposed. I felt undone, unlearned, ineffective, and above all, broken. I felt the pain of my child's inability to understand, why did this happen?

I have taken the necessary actions for my family, and the healing process has taken place. I will always be in a posture of healing until the day I leave this earth. I am nervous, and somewhat uncertain, of all that I will be disclosing in this book. I know one thing for certain is my God will get the glory out of this book. I didn't write my experience for pity or to bring shame. This is the only way some of us will get the message, which is, we need to seek the wisdom of God. One common factor, in all humanity, is we all identify with hurt, shame, pain, embarrassment and turmoil, of every kind, known to mankind. I will give God the glory for bringing me through this violation in my family structure. I bring this kind of writing to fruition and exposure to release every prisoner. The prisoner who thinks everything that has ever gone wrong in life was their fault. I introduce to you my real-life story.

I know what has happened is real. I know it is real because I didn't hear my baby crying. You may ask the question, why didn't you hear your baby? The bible tells us that my people perish for the lack of knowledge. I had not been acclimated to a family member being vile and abusive, physically nor sexually, to another family member. I didn't have spiritual insight to such activity in the body of humanity. I didn't see any signs of this kind in my home. I feel the need to move forward and go into the writing of a lifetime. The life of a mother and woman of faith, did I forget to tell you that part? Yes, I am a woman of faith in Jesus the son of God. I am also grateful to be a delivered drug addict. I have been clean and made whole now for 32 years. The onset of the life of this book began in May of 1996. The song writer composed a song, "If I could turn back the hands of time." I often say these lyrics. If I knew then what I know now, knowing what I know now, I know things would have been different. I just thank almighty God for bringing my children and I out, now walking in healing, forgiveness and wholeness. The first chapter will bring a brief, however detailed, summary of the beginning of the end of a place in my life. I will be very direct. I recognize this is not what Big Mama would want, but Big Mama got to tell her story. This is the final dose of medicine for the pain that someone who declared they loved me caused.

I expressed that I am a Christian. I am born again. I want you all to remember that I walked with the Lord through every circumstance and situation you will read. I had come to a place unknowingly, where I would tell my testimony. I was on a tele-conference line. Someone that day was going through somewhat of the same ordeal I had experienced. When I had the opportunity, and my nerves didn't stop me, I asked to speak. When I told my testimony of my husband at the time, my children, and many were in awe.

DR. APOSTLE ROBBIE CARSWELL

I remember making a statement that I didn't know, or see anything showing this was going on. I didn't recognize it until the Lord began to reveal it in dreams and visions which caused me to seek out what God wanted me to know. "I could not believe that Prophetess Robbie Carswell told her secret." I was almost in a state of waiting to exhale. Then the visionary of the line came on. This is what he shared. He stated, "You knew." I responded, "I didn't grow up in a house where mom and dad did things or allowed inappropriate touching or dressing to act out." I emphasized and told everyone listening that I didn't know until God showed me what was going on in dreams and visions. Then the prophet gave me a prophetic word. This is the prophecy which was released. He prophesied that God was going to bless me when I write my book; it is going to bless a rich Caucasian woman. He professed that when she read my book, it is going to release her from the prison she has been locked in since she was raped. He affirmed this book will bring healing to a certain Caucasian woman who would be a great blessing. He also proclaimed this book would release her to give a great donation. I am not writing this book for the riches. I am writing to bring ministry and reconciliation to the woman who has been silent too long. This prophecy acknowledged this book is also telling her life story. God bless you all.

GO
UP
WITH
US

www.GoUpWithUs.com

-Foreword-

It is an honor to publish this book by a wonderful Christian woman. Transparency is never easy when it's exposing and bringing things into the light which have been kept in the dark for many years. I'm an author who has trademarked my books with transparency from my first book, and with many books which followed. I commend Robbie for sharing her story which will bring healing, freedom, and joy to those who will be delivered from their abusive traumas. The best is yet to come for her, her family, her readers, in the name of Jesus. Amen.

Marcus L. Boston

AUTHOR – CEO UNFAZED PUBLISHING

-TABLE OF CONTENTS-

I

Didn't

HEAR

My Baby

CRYING

DR. APOSTLE ROBBIE CARSWELL

UNFAZED PUBLISHING
YOUR MIND IS OUR BUSINESS

TAMPA FLORIDA

CHAPTER ONE

<u>"THE CASE IS CLOSED"</u>

I am at the onset of a new chapter in my life. I have just gone to court pertaining to the custody of my children. I never thought being before a judge would feel as rewarding as it does. I feel so empowered and confident that I will do a great job providing and loving on my children. No more will anyone tell me when and how long I can be in the presence of my children.

I have completed an intensive outpatient care drug recovery program. It was a year and 6-months of dedication. I was mandated by the court system with the Department of Children and Family Services. I had an addiction to cocaine. My use of drugs and alcohol caused the consequences which led to the temporary custody loss of my children. The choice I made landed me in trouble with the state as some would say. I cannot be more grateful. I thank God for somebody getting in my business to help me gain stability and management of my life again. I also had to undergo random drug screens. Completing a drug addiction recovery program was serious business. I even had to prove I was seeking gainful employment. I had much to do to get my children back.

I attended self-help groups with other recovering drug addicts and had to sign an attendance sheet each meeting. This was my new routine and lifestyle on the road to having custody again. I did everything recommended and ordered by the state. I complied with my case manager and completed each task she charted in my case. I worked diligently until I began to notice my life transforming into something which I had not been accustomed to for a long time. It was called being normal. I finally obtained a job which wasn't much. It was a warehouse job handling mail, but I really enjoyed working with my hands. I had a perfect attendance record at work, never late, and faithful to my state ordered meetings as well. I made up my mind I wanted to live a normal life, and I wanted the privilege of having my parental rights reinstated by the court.

I never felt so overwhelmed at getting to work and making my required meetings until now. I was very angry at the beginning of this process. I was also afraid of being kicked out of some familiar places because I told many people, who hung with me, my situation. I knew when I stopped being invited to get high anymore, that this transformation was seriously real. I couldn't get high anymore. The people who used to sell it to me backed away from me, and guess what? No one else would sell it to me. Everything was shaping itself into my favor to regain my children. I was beginning to go with the flow of this new place in my life and the anger I had began to cease as my life reshaped itself. My appearance also began to be brighter, and I started looking better, healthier, and happier as my life continued to change positively.

I completed my probationary period on my job. I secured my bag as they say nowadays. However, I had a new assignment, or task, from my DCFS case worker. I was informed with news I really didn't care to hear. I was told

I couldn't keep my visitation with my children if I continued living in a home where anyone was actively using drugs. I had to find another place to live. I had to remove myself from people, and places that indulged in any type of drug use. I began thinking of where I could live where no one used drugs. It was then, at this very moment, the Lord brought to my mind my brother's girlfriend. I never had any contact with her, but I had to gain enough courage to ask her if I could rent a room at her residence. I remembered she had a very large, renovated basement with a private bath and shower. I contacted her and shared everything I was experiencing. I passionately told her how I wanted to regain my parental rights and get custody of my children. She was more than willing to help me. I moved into her drug free home, I could clearly see my life, at this time, was being orchestrated by God. My old life was dying, and my new life was being developed. I was now in a place of stability and learning to be independent again. I know it was the grace of God that I made it this far.

Although I knew I was growing, there were so many pitfalls and snares that I could speak of during this time. My recovery was a breath-to-breath experience. God was breathing new life into me. He was my mouth-to-mouth lifeforce. I was determined to complete my drug recovery program and learn to live drug free. I continued working at the warehouse and faithfully attending my meetings. I realized all things work together for the good of them that love the Lord and the called according to his purpose. This bible verse is Romans chapter 8

Verse 28. I cannot believe how far I've come in such a short time. Nevertheless, I am enjoying this process now. My anger is now behind me and it feels good to have a smile on my face once again.

I have been faithful in everything the legal system has mandated me to do. I knew in my heart something was pulling for my attention. It wasn't a desire to get high pulling on me. The Spirit of God began to draw me back to the church. Before I left the church, I was taught to attend and listen to the preached word of God. I was taught to pay my tithes, and I placed ten percent of my paycheck in an envelope every pay period to give to God. I could feel God drawing me back, but I was resisting His call. I did not go through the church doors just yet. I knew God was causing a yearning for Him to return inside of me. I knew I would soon attend a church service because of this drawing. This longing for church pulled on my heart every day. I recalled the days when my soul was delighting in the presence of the Lord. I didn't know when I would return to church, but I knew it was soon, very soon.

In the midst of my lifestyle change, I honored God although I wasn't going to church. I trusted His Hand because I understood it was His grace that was reconstructing my life. I was saving my tithes although I wasn't going to church. I remember, one day in December, I purposed in my heart to finally attend a worship service. At this time, I almost had a year of tithes saved on my nightstand. I grabbed the money and pressed my way to church. I had a wonderful time at church and it was a great feeling to give God the tithes I was saving just for Him. How refreshing it was to be in the house of God once again.

As I continued going to church, I now recognized I was awakened from a somewhat dead zone. I was coming out of a life of being numb and disconnected with my emotions. I could now relate to my feelings and my hurt. I wasn't rushing this process at all. At this point, I knew I was transforming into a new creature in Christ Jesus. At my church, I began to enjoy myself in worship, and I attended our services as often as I could. I am well on my way. I thought nothing could go wrong with the Lord orchestrating my life so well. Things in my life were manageable and pretty much under control. I did not have a mindset, at any time, to take anything for granted. Nor did I fool myself into thinking that I didn't need help from anyone anymore. I began concentrating on the power, presence, and will of God to keep me clean from drugs. I embraced our worship service and the preached Word of God. I transitioned back to my good home rearing and identified this was a time of refreshing for me. This was a very good season in my life.

I was working very hard to gain visitation with my children again. I was grateful the process was going well, and I knew I had to be very patient. I did everything from beginning to end the state told me to do. This is how the DCFS (Department of Children and Family Services) works. I was finally given one hour a week with supervised visitation with my kids.

Moreover, I had to take random drug tests, so the state knew there were no substances in my system. They wanted to make sure I wasn't still using drugs. I continued with these conditions until I finally gained one hour with unsupervised visitation. I displayed good character with each supervised visit and was rewarded with unsupervised time. This was a big milestone for me and this transition I was going through. I didn't have to have anyone monitor and document every detail of my time with my kids. It was very awkward at times. I remember telling my children, "Mommy is going to bring you all home." I never let our visits end without reminding them that I loved them, and we were going to be back together again. They all responded, "Good Mommy," in their own way. It's amazing my younger kids had more hope and expectations than I did at one time. It hurt me to see what my life had caused, yet I had a mind to correct, rebuild, and recover from every bad mistake I made. I could not have done it without the help of my pastor, the mothers of the church, and my friends who were not using drugs. I was very thankful.

CHAPTER TWO

"<u>COMING HOME</u>"

I am actually doing this. I have made it through some of the greatest challenges with my recovery. The key for me was to keep it simple and not lose my focus. I looked good, and I felt wonderful drug free. My life was unfolding with many opportunities. My children and I were on our way to being reunited permanently. During this time, I met a young man, and we started dating. Now I have never had a relationship while being sober. I began spending time with him on a regular basis. My dating experience didn't interfere with anything in my life. We dated until we had a very close relationship. One day we started being intimate. I was sexually active with him and later found myself pregnant. The

DCFS representative handling my case started watching me closely again. I wasn't using any drugs with this pregnancy, but they gave me more random drug tests just to be sure. I tried not to let this bother me. They were only making sure I stayed on track, and this was actually a good thing.

The birth of this baby created another chapter in my life. My daughter was born clean and healthy. No trace of any drugs in her system. I called her my breakthrough baby. The nurses and doctors knew me from my previous deliveries. They were happy for me. The hospital staff came to my room after she was born sharing their joyful thoughts with me. They knew I lost custody of my other children. The nursing staff gave me their personal numbers and volunteered to keep in touch. I thanked God for them. They were so proud of me. I was, and still is, proud of myself too. The Department of Children and Family Services made their initial visit, and no other case was opened. I was so grateful I didn't lose custody of my new baby. I just had to complete my only open case. I was particularly happy I received a great report written concerning my participation with my program and recovery.

The father of my newborn daughter asked me to marry him because he wanted to do what was right. I have never been married. I was thinking about the well-being of my family and thought of my children having a father figure within our home. I said yes to his marriage proposal. After our engagement, I began having outings with our extended family so we could all get to know each other. I continued going to my church faithfully and nothing hindered my case. I want to take the time here to remind you that I have never had a relationship before without drug usage. This was my first relationship in my adult life without drugs being involved. I made up my mind I would never need to go through DCFS ever again. I meant that with a vengeance! I made a vow to God, if He keep me clean and sober, that I would live a whole new life for Him. With God's help, I have been sober and free from mind-altering and mood-altering substances for about three years now.

My fiancé and I began to talk more about getting married. I knew it wasn't right to have a child out of wedlock. I wanted to be married if I was going to continue having a relationship with him. I didn't push him, nor did I manipulate him. I continued going to church and praying for God to bless my children and me. I prayed that God would touch my fiancé's heart to do right by me. I really want you to truly understand why I just told you this. Well, you see, I already had 4 children, and their fathers didn't talk about marrying me because of my drug use. I can't blame them at all as I reflect on this today. It was very strongly within my heart to start being faithful to God and be in better standing with Him. I wanted to please the Lord. I didn't want to experience the same things I did in my past relationships. God has been so good to me, and I desired to be good to Him. Speaking of God being good to me. Well, guess what? The case with the state is now over. I was granted custody of my children, and the case is now closed. Glory to

God. I am totally free and at liberty to raise my kids freely without repercussions. I was so happy to have the support of DCFS to raise all my children together. I wanted them to have a mother and father in the same home as I did. I can't deny my feelings for this man, my fiancé, are growing too. He and I are bonding more and more each day. In my pursuit to please God, I stopped having sex with my fiancé and hoped he'd understand or at least respect my walk with God. This was a real struggle for me knowing how pleasing it was to be with him intimately. I resisted him until I couldn't any longer. I had another sexual encounter with my fiancé. I finally made up my mind that I will not keep sinning sexually and failing God. I seriously dedicated my life to the Lord. I welcomed and rededicated my life to Jesus

Christ. I repented of all my sins and asked Him to be my Lord and personal Savior.

I soon began to look for a new job to help with the raising of our family. I found a night job so I would be available for my children in the daytime. I wanted to be available for Parent -Teacher Conferences and get to know their teachers. I desired to pick up their report cards and hear their teacher's feedback so I can help or assist in a specific way with homework. My mother was my childcare provider, and I appreciate the delicate manner she had with children.

It took a little while before we got married, but that day finally arrived. We got married and I won't share any details. My husband moved into my apartment with us and this was an adjustment, but a good one. As a new wife,

I maintained our life as it would be pleasing to God. I kept a clean house and cooked for my family. I catered to my husband and made sure he was pleased. When my husband moved in with us, he didn't bring all his things. We visited his apartment until he managed to put most of his things in storage and transitioned into our home with his family. He had a decent job position at a respected company. I went to school to become a Certified Nursing Assistant. This paid more than the warehouse job and I thought this was a good idea. I had the heart to be a good wife, and desired to help my husband with finances. I did the laundry on my days off and spent quality time with my children. My mom was a great example of a wife. I learned a lot from her experiences with our family. I prayed to be a good wife and God has taught me how to be a wife and mother. I said mother because I'm free of drugs now and honestly, all of this is new to me without using drugs. I desired to be available, as much as I could, for my children and show them how much I love them daily. My children, from the oldest to the youngest, were remarkable. I appreciated God for blessing me with them all. Their ages were 8, 5, 3, 2, and 1.

My mother helped me with my kids. I don't know what I would have done without her being in my life. The Department of Children and Family Services awarded my family a financial grant to help us with our reunification and needs for our new start. This was a tremendous blessing. With this money, we got a better apartment and were able to buy new furniture. All things were truly becoming new. I was very happy during this time. The father of my previous children was a great help in his children's lives as well. This was a good season. Our first Christmas was very memorable. We celebrated every birthday, every holiday, and all was well as our first two years have gone by.

One day, I came in from work as my husband was preparing to go to work. I asked if he would join us on Sunday and we go to church together as a family. He declined. He didn't want to attend church for a while. I didn't push him, yet loved on him, and left that to him and God. He was a man that never used drugs or alcohol, he brought his whole check home and helped me with all our children. He also helped with his children he fathered before we were together. I thanked God for showing me how to handle the stress which comes with a pretty big family. God knows the adjustment had some issues.

The good part of our adjustment was I didn't have the state interfering with my relationship with my children. No longer was I under their rules and regulations. One big adjustment was managing all their attitudes and defusing sibling rivalries. I had to teach them how to get along in a healthy way, but I didn't mind doing this at all. It was an honor to be functioning as their mom with each and every one of them. No complaints here. In my childhood, I was raised in a Christian home, and as an adult I am living a willing Christian life. No one is forcing it on me. I really understand the difference and the commitment.

Well, one day, my husband entered our apartment asking me if our neighbor was home. I really didn't know if they were or not. He then asked me to let him know when I saw him because He wanted a haircut. When I finally saw this neighbor, I informed him. He went over right away. The next thing I know was my husband coming through the doors with a fresh haircut. His head was shaved, and his beard was cut completely off. He was totally clean cut. "Oh my God," I thought as my husband was looking so good to me. This sight gave me the best feeling in the world. I believe God gave me this feeling and I rejoiced seeing my clean-cut husband.

This was the beginning of a prayer being answered. I saw that God has touched the heart of my husband, and he has stepped into the place of headship. He took the first step with becoming a Christian. He made the decision on his own. Seeing him give his life to Jesus blessed my soul. What a wonderful day this was in my eyes. He made it to church as often as he could when he didn't have to work overtime. Finally, we went to church as a family. I loved this so much. Sitting together in our congregation as a complete family felt amazing. I didn't like when members asked, "Where is your husband?" or "When is your husband coming to church?" They now smiled as we walked in together. It seemed like everything was going as smoothly as ever. I could not see anything going wrong. I have a good husband, I see my children growing up with one getting ready to leave for college full-time. All was truly well, and I gave God the praise with each passing day.

I can't believe it's December 1998, and I'm about to have another baby. This is the birth of my sixth child. I am married, my husband and I are in church together, and we are bringing in two incomes home. My husband and I had a budget together. All money was accounted for. I couldn't ask for a better life. We were not perfect, but we were working together. I never imagined an injury would have me down for a little while. Yea, I experienced my first on the job injury which caused me to need surgery. The bright side of this was that I could be at home with my smaller children and give my mother a break from babysitting. I am the kind of person who really missed being at home with my children. I just didn't like being at a disadvantage with the pain from my injury. I had to force myself to sit down so I could heal properly. I always wanted to help as much as I could, but my body needed its proper rest so I could not only return to work totally healed, but assist within our home like I used to do.

CHAPTER THREE

"THE BATHROOM DOOR"

I had surgery on my right elbow. I was off my job for about four weeks and could return being on light duty. As I was dealing with my recovery, I realized a lot of things happen with six children in a two-bedroom apartment. We as parents understand things get broken with many children. Because I had young children, I had an early bathing schedule for my little ones. I started with the youngest first and had my older children help me with them. This made me free to finish cleaning and do other things in our house. As we continued using our bathroom, the doorknob on the bathroom door became so loose I could see inside the bathroom. I taught my sons to respect their sisters. They knew to turn their heads and keep their eyes away from seeing them dressing or using the toilet.

I taught them, as their mother, things which were not acceptable and not to let anyone touch them. I began teaching them good touches and bad touches. I let my children know if anyone touches you in a way which made them feel bad to tell me. I told them, "Mommy would not ever touch certain areas and nobody else should either. Please don't never be afraid to tell me."

One day I told my husband, "Honey, I need you to fix the bathroom door. I already taught the kids that when the girls are in the bathtub, the boys are to stay away from the bathroom. I supervised them and there was no confusion about it." He didn't get up and fix it. He said he would get to it. I wanted the doorknob fixed in that instant, but at least he said he would do it.

My oldest daughter was 8 years old, and she was beginning to develop her breasts. I was really mindful of her development, as I knew she would be having her first menstrual cycle soon. One day while my oldest daughter was taking her bath, I knocked on the door and told her I would wash the tub when she was finished. My younger daughter would knock on the bathroom door if she had to use it. My oldest daughter would tell her to come in. I heard her scream, "Close the door!" to her little sister. I could tell by her scream that I had to go see what happened. After I arrived at our bathroom, I asked, "Can I come in?" My oldest daughter replied, "Yea Mommy." After I entered, she stated, "Mom, dad saw me." I responded, "He saw you naked? The door wasn't open that long. I came as soon as I heard you scream." I explained to her that her sister closed the door quickly. I will never forget how she looked at me and expressed, "No Mom, Dad saw me." I saw the look on my daughter's face, and I knew she felt very uncomfortable. You know the look someone gives you (when they tell you) that someone saw something they shouldn't have? My daughter had the beginning lumps forming her breast. I told her, "I will talk to him and tell him that you saw him look at you." I wanted to assure her that he didn't mean to. I took no thought, at the time, that something had taken place I could not see with the natural eye. I went to my husband. I talked with him about my daughter's concern and how she felt. The moment I shared what my daughter told me, he said he didn't look at her, and that he was just passing by the bathroom door. I discussed my daughter's feelings toward him. He replied, "Aww, I didn't see anything." I was angry! I saw how my daughter looked! She clearly felt like he had no business looking at her. She looked as if he saw her in a certain way. A way no grown man should ever look at a little girl. Every mother knows the feeling I felt when I heard my daughter's voice. I had to restore all of my daughter's dignity, no matter what. I immediately called the maintenance man, had the bathroom door fixed, and a lock placed on the inside again. My daughter gained her since of privacy again. She was back to going in and out of the bathroom without worrying if anyone could or would see her. She was safely locked inside. This will not happen again, and I was happy my baby could be at peace.

I was still healing from my surgery and loving being an at home mom. I realized being at home with my children was great. I know we couldn't make it with 6 children and only one income. I had to return to work and help get my family financially back on track. The children had to be in the tub by 8:00pm and in bed by 9:00 pm. My work schedule was from 11:00pm until 7:00 am. I finally received a work release form from my doctor to return to work for light duty. Working light duty will have me on the day shift. My husband didn't realize that I didn't have to go work overnight. I noticed within a 6-week time span, he was getting my oldest daughter to wash the dishes alone in the kitchen. He explained it was time for her to start helping around the house. He also began telling my 6-year-old son, the oldest boy, to start taking the garbage out. I thought this was appropriate, and I agreed with my husband.

As time was going by and it became more unbearable to work after surgery, I took off to heal and get physical therapy. Light duty was still too much for my arm. One day I was taking a power nap. My nap was disturbed by the voice of my husband calling my oldest daughter. I heard him tell her to get in the kitchen or he was going to tell on her. I didn't pay any attention to the children getting corrected and directed to do their chores until this happened. I was lying down with my bedroom door open. I saw my daughter getting up from her bed on a school night. I heard the tone my husband had with her. This caused me to sit up. I saw her face. She really didn't want to go into the kitchen. As I was sitting up, I told my daughter to go back to bed and said I would clean the kitchen. I saw the relief on her face. I didn't have an alarm in my spirit about cleaning the kitchen. I had an alarm about him telling her he was going to tell on her. What happened in the kitchen? I thought my daughter had broken a dish, a glass, or something. What was he using to get her to wash dishes by manipulation? It was something but I knew it didn't make sense. I needed an answer.

I was off work for 6 weeks for physical therapy. I told my children I would be home and take them to school. I was still faithful with my walk of faith, but all of a sudden, my husband stops going to church. A few days of missed church turned into more services being missed. I found myself going to church with my children alone again. I really didn't mind, but now I was receiving those same questions again. When my husband stopped attending church, I started noticing my oldest daughter would give him a report of everything when we returned home. I had to speak to her on several occasions. I thought, "What does she think she's doing? She better get in her place." I started correcting her about telling everything to him. I told her she needed to mind her business. As I corrected her, my attention was redirected because I recognized a more than a child's attitude. I openly told her I do not allow her to communicate like this to him. I didn't want her to be conditioned to telling everything as a job of sort. I wanted her to know that if anything was to be addressed, it would come from me and not from her. I reminded my daughter of her role as a child and what she should be doing in a child's place. I believed because she was developing and starting puberty, her attitude was changing. I had to be mildly stern with her. I believe all kids go through some kind of personality change. I know this for sure with girls. She was even dressing differently. I thought it was because she realized her change in life and was growing up. I had no idea why this sudden change was occurring. I really thought it was all accounted to her just growing up. I recall the phrase my old folk used to say, "The young girl just smelling herself." This only means in small talk, she was growing up fast.

I loved watching over my children. I watched them when they played outside, and I never left them alone or unattended. Remember my case with DCFS? Well, I sure didn't want another case with them ever again. I didn't want DCFS in my life by any stretch of my imagination. There is something really pulling on my heart now. I remember my daughter was given some clothes from one of the members of our church. I accepted them because I had a big family. I gave birth to 4 girls and 2 boys. We needed all the help we could get. This donation was very helpful, and I appreciated it. However, I noticed that my daughter was beginning to wear some things I felt was too open at the top and was something for an older woman. I know because she didn't have the fullness to wear these clothes yet. My daughter is still a growing girl. I sewed up the sides and made it fit more comfortably on her. Now I felt more comfortable knowing she was covered up properly and looking like a young lady.

CHAPTER FOUR

<u>"Mom, My Leg Hurts"</u>

I sat at the door of our house one day. My oldest daughter was getting up slowly this morning. My third oldest child is now going to school with them, and I only had the youngest 3 at home. I have almost one year and a half, and all my children will be school. Today, as my oldest daughter was getting ready for school, I asked her if she was feeling well. She answered, "Mommy my leg hurt. I asked if she fell while playing. She replied to me, "No Mom." My oldest daughter was now in the fourth grade. I asked if she wanted to stay at home. I watched her walk down the stairs and across the field which led to the paved path headed for school. I looked at my daughter closely. She looked as if her leg was really hurt as she walked with a limp. I had no idea of what was being revealed to me in my obscurity.

I began watching my daughter more closely. I noticed her getting up slower and slower. At least she always had a willingness to go to school. She took her time though. Her brother would always fuss at her for being slow yelling, "COME ON!" with urgency to his sister. I knew this was how a brother and sister acted together when the oldest was a girl. It was always a power play in a fun way.

I now had a concern about my daughter. I knew the time of her menstrual cycle was very close, but I didn't understand why her leg was hurting. Did she fall while riding her bike? Did she fall while playing with her friends or siblings? Why is her leg hurting? I didn't understand. I didn't hear her crying. Then out of nowhere it seemed, her leg wasn't hurting anymore. She walked around, ran, and played with no mention of pain anymore. I thought her leg healed all on its own. I decided to take some time off from work and tend more to my family. This was my motherly decision to be with my kids.

My plan was to keep the upper hand so my children would not get away from the discipline format I structured. I truly enjoyed being in full time mom mode again. The Lord has been so gracious to us. Well, as you know, a mother's job is never done. I had to start buying new clothes again. My kids were growing up and needed new clothes & shoes. I have always been resourceful. The understanding my husband and I agreed on

DR. APOSTLE ROBBIE CARSWELL

was he paid the rent and bills, and I took care
of the kids clothing, school supplies, and a few
other things. I have been at home for a while
now and feel my children can adjust to me
going back to work. I liked the overnight shift
and understood I could be at home for my kids
if they needed me throughout the day. I know
I asked for it, but things got a little noisy. Once
again, I had to adjust to getting some sleep
before my shift. My oldest daughter and my
oldest son knew to do their chores. We have
gone through this before. As I was laying
down, I heard my husband reminding my
daughter to get up and wash the dishes. My
husband called her very sternly. I saw her
looking very sleepy. I asked her, as she was
passing by my bedroom door, "Why didn't
you clean up before you went to bed." She

answered, "I did." Now I am wondering why he is waking her up. She had already cleaned the kitchen. My husband was a stickler about anything left on the stove or any little thing out of place. I thought this was why he was being so strict about the kitchen being cleaned. I knew my children needed to be asleep before I left for work. I checked our kitchen every night to make sure everything was clean. Eventually he wasn't waking her up on a school night anymore, but heard my daughter saying to herself almost laughing, "Mom to the rescue." She was very happy she didn't have to get up anymore. I am happy the kitchen is not a problem anymore.

I was in our house one day. Just my daughter and me. The strangest thought came to my mind. I turned to her and asked, "Why was Dad so hard on you about the kitchen?" I also asked her, "And what did he mean about, 'I'm gonna tell your momma on you?'" I noticed her whole-body language changed. I felt as if she was keeping something from me or just didn't want me to tell me. She replied, "He just wanted me to come and wash a fork or a spoon." I didn't like that, and it made me angry! I called my kids together again. I told them, "The house rules are changing. From now on, the only room you all will have to clean is your bedroom." I wanted to troubleshoot this issue with a drill sergeant mentality. The joy on their faces was priceless to see. I knew what I said was on point and the stress or pressure, to help keep a cleaned home, lifted off my children.

One day, during the weekend, my husband

called me to ask if my daughter could go with him to his side hustle. He picked up toys for children to sell. I thought this was his way of making up for being so hard on her. I am not a funny acting woman. One thing I do not do is have favorites between my children. When they returned home, she had a large stuffed animal. The other girls got something very contrary to this toy. I didn't feel it was equal. Either you give them all the same, or equal toy, or no one gets one. I asked my daughter where they went. She answered, "Dad went to his friend and picked up the toys, and he sold some and we came home." She looked like she had a nice time, however, the life of a mother is never on vacation. I cleared up this situation when I told my husband my expectations. I shared with him, "You will not take one child

with you again. You must take all of them."
After I declared this to my husband, my
daughter didn't go anywhere else with him
alone, and he never took all of the children.

We've had many issues, but I made it
through another year of raising my children.
Every now and then, I reflect on what my
major concerns were with these kids. I thought
about things with school and their friends. I
was basically doing a wellness check with
them. My youngest son was being more
watchful and paying attention to everything.
His time to start going to school was getting
close. He was very keen to observe anything
and everything. Something caught my
attention with him. When my son hears my
husband's car pull into the driveway, he has a
certain reaction. He jumps up and looks out the

window. His demeanor changes from being his happy go lucky self, to being a blank kind of look. Then he would be off and out of sight. At first, I thought this was happening because my husband is not their biological father. Maybe this was an issue my children had with him. I came to realize this wasn't the case.

My second oldest daughter was very close to her grandmother; my mom. I didn't want to break that bond since my mother was so very instrumental in helping me regain custody of my family. I allowed my daughter and mother to continue spending as much time together as they desired. I also recognized the affection my daughter had for my mom. I saw how she missed being away from her granny. She never let a day go by without checking on her granny. I knew if this relationship was broken it would cause my daughter to feel detachment depression. I did what any mother would do, and that was allowing her to remain with my mother. Whenever she wanted to come home and be with us, we welcomed her with open arms. It was fine with me, and this actually worked out because my kids were beginning to have less space with all their belongings slowly increasing.

Having custody of my children and being free of drugs has been a loving journey. Seeing them growing and their personalities developing has been very interesting. With one child living with my mother, things in our home were settling again in a different way. Plus, I have another child off to kindergarten, and he is excited. I began reflecting on things each of my children were facing and their behavior. We have come a long way in such a short time. I know the kids are mindful of their stepdad in the house and his ways. We will have to move soon as the children are out growing our apartment. I was glad in a way. With so many things being needed within our apartment and our children, I went back to work.

There were no issues until my sleep was broken on my first day off. I heard my husband calling my oldest daughter. He sounded forceful! He told her to get up and take a shower. I immediately jumped up and asked why. I focused my attention on my husband. I asked him, "Why does she have to take a shower?" I was very upset because we have structure with such a large family. When my daughter got up, there was a difference in her appearance. Her hair was all over her head like she had been in a fight. I realized that by working the night shift, I don't see her when she first gets up. I told my husband I would get them together. He had to go to work. I didn't think something was wrong. I didn't feel my daughter would break a house rule without a good reason. My reason for saying this is because she knows how I feel about them being clean and bathed. This is a pet peeve of mine. This situation started my husband and I to disagree a lot. The kitchen wasn't an issue anymore, but he started calling my oldest daughter about other things. Whatever he asked her to do, I did it. I felt he wasn't being fair. She was not the only child in our family who could help out. I began to stand up to him rather forcefully each time he called her. I felt he wasn't giving her liberty to be a little girl and have the same fun as her siblings. The rest of my family didn't see anything wrong with it, but I certainly did. Why doesn't he call on my oldest son? He didn't interact much with him. However, when he was asked to do something, he did what he was told and was out of the way. My husband didn't like me telling my daughter to go play outside while I cleaned up, folded the clothes, or whatever he was calling her constantly for.

One day the arguing started and became increasingly more daily. I will not allow my husband to treat my child this way. I felt he was being too controlling and hard for no reason. In the long run, we began to have heated verbal fights about it, and I did not compromise. My husband decided to go back to his apartment, and yes, he still has this apartment.

I cut my days at work to be with my family again. I started cleaning up the kid's room since my husband was not in the house. I changed many things. I was able to get new furniture, and I gave the boys the bedroom they shared with their sisters. The girls came into my bedroom. My husband would visit us with his children, and this routine was fine with me. We were separated for about a month when my husband came back home. I went back to work full-time when my twin sister moved into the same building on the first floor. I have a stronger network now if I needed to work more hours and I thanked the Lord.

As I cleaned up our apartment, I found my kid's dirty socks and underwear hiding under the bed and in their toy box. I had to stay on my children concerning this. They hated doing laundry. My boy's socks used to really stink. This wasn't the worse thing I discovered. Next, I found my oldest daughter's panties hidden behind the drawer. This really sent an alarm because this was not normal. A few dirty socks on the floor are not an issue with small kids, but hidden panties made me ponder. I pulled them out and thought, "Why would she hide her underwear?" I waited until she was home from school so we could talk about it. They all knew when I cleaned up, I cleaned everywhere. I washed their clothing, cleaned the closet, the toy box, the shoe box, and everything. I do this so that no one will have mixed match socks etc. However, even though they knew I would clean everything, this I noted on the butt part of her underwear, there was blood. I thought for sure it was from her period. She recently said she had pain when she used the bathroom. I thought it was constipation and gave her over the counter stool softener. She told me the medicine helped her, and this concern wasn't a problem anymore since the pain had ceased. This was nothing compared to what happened next.

I had an appointment at a resource center and told my kids I would take them to school a little early. After I dropped them off at school and finished my appointment, I returned home. I started cleaning up and this is when I saw something which was frightening. I went into my bedroom looking at a red line on the side of my bed's comforter. At first, I thought it was spilled punch. I even looked to see if my period came on and I didn't know it. I began getting angry at the thought of my husband being unfaithful and having some woman on her period, in my bed, while I was at work. I pulled the comforter back along with the sheets. The stain didn't go through. So, he had some woman in my bed who bled on my comforter. I never could have imagined what would come out of this ordeal.

I heard the key in the door as my husband was coming inside our apartment. I called him and told him that I had to talk to him right then and there. I didn't keep my voice down to keep the neighbors from hearing this discussion. I was at the top of my lungs asking, "WHO DID YOU HAVE IN MY BED!!!??? I KNOW A WOMAN WAS IN MY BED BLEEDING!!!" I showed him the stain. He couldn't deny it. He would not tell me who it was, but he kept saying he was so sorry. I told him to get out and don't come back. I told my kids don't open the door for him. I asked my sister downstairs to care for my kids when I went to work.

The trust was gone in my marriage, and I never wanted to see him ever again. My only desire at this point was to take care of my children. I had no choice but to continue working through this situation. I had the only income now. I was still extremely frustrated by the fact that another woman had been in my bed. I thought, "How could my husband bring another woman in our bedroom, and she was on her period?" How nasty can that be? The very thought of it was going through my mind daily. I couldn't wrap my mind around the fact that my husband had another woman in our bed. I thought I was enough for him. I mean, look at me. Aren't I attractive and curvy? Many men find me attractive. I was faithful! I fulfilled my responsibility as his wife. I mean, we had a very enjoyable sex life. I knew our sex life was not a problem between the two of us. I am trying to keep it together as I am recalling these events. My bed never felt the same.

Although I was hurting deeply, I continued being faithful to my commitment at my local worship assembly. I needed the strength from almighty God to help me. I knew that He would strengthen me. "Why?" is the question that keeps coming to my mind. If I could only get "a peace" about why he betrayed our marriage vows. I must move on from this state of mind. (I need the Lord to help me right now because it is getting painful to write about this.

I know I must finish this book. I feel like my heart is in a great big knot. Let me go on with this release of my truth.)

My family and I have regained our sense of unity and security without my husband being present. I yet have this nagging thought afflicting my mind. I cannot tell you the time or date of the very first thought. I can, however, tell you what the thought was about. I was sitting in the living room one day. It was the summer school break for my children. My oldest daughter was coming in from outside taking a break from the heat. I asked her to come to where I was located. I wanted so badly to ask her if my husband had another woman in our house while I was away at work. Then I thought, "How could I involve my child in an adult situation?" I couldn't do it. So, I just told her, "Never mind. Just go back and play outside."

This is the onset of supernatural intervention as I began to cast all of my cares and give this situation to the Lord. Yes, I cried many nights this far, but I kept asking God to reveal what was going on in my home. I asked the Lord to take control of my life. I honestly didn't have any rest spiritually. I didn't talk about the things which went on in my home. I only prayed. I thanked God as he began to show me certain things. As I prayed, God started giving me dreams. I didn't understand them at first. I didn't understand them then like I do right now. I didn't have the knowledge I have today on spiritual warfare, bondage, or mind control. Now I am in the trenches with the Lord and being hand taught how to fight in the Spirit for my family. I can remember these dreams as if they were given to me yesterday. I'm going to share my dreams with you and there is no beauty in them either. Please pray with me as I share. These dreams came to me with signs and wonders, and a very painful revelation.

CHAPTER FIVE

"THE BEGINNING OF WISDOM"

The Lord has been giving me dreams. I am sharing them in the order they were given to me. During the time my husband was gone, I prayed. The first dream I had started with me going down the road. I was driving and the children were in the back seat. I looked to the left, and thought, "Don't stop. This area doesn't look right." As I drove my car, the people standing or looking on my left side, made me feel they were not good individuals. I then started looking on my right side. I saw a person who looked familiar to me. I had a thought which made me feel I had known him, and it was good a good feeling. But a man I knew saw me and started to walk toward my car. I watched as he faced me. His whole body changed into the form of an animal. As the young man was approaching my car, his features changed. I felt afraid and yelled out to my children. I urgently shouted to close the windows. Wind them up. (Our car didn't have power windows) I was persistent and repeated myself, "Close the windows!" I locked the doors. I pulled off but couldn't drive forward like I wanted to because I was looking in the back seat at my oldest daughter. I noticed she couldn't wind up the window because she was looking at the man coming to our car. Her focus was on the man. She was panicking and was slow about getting the window closed. I asked, "Is it all the way up?" Then I woke up from my dream. I didn't see any of my other children once my focus turned to my oldest daughter. It was a strange realization that I did not comprehend at that time. In this dream my only concern was with my oldest daughter. I began praying to God for a better understanding. I understood most of my dream, but I desired the full meaning.

I continued to allow my children to play outside and enjoy themselves. The time apart from my husband was healing many things. The man that was supposed to be a role model, and a father figure, was found to be a cheater. He is out of my life. I allowed him, while I was home, to visit his children I had with him. Well, I still had a job and didn't need his assistance. The strength of my stance, at this point, was due to the fact that God was my sustainer and provider. Now this is the end and the beginning. Let me give an interpretation. My dream was letting me know of something that was going to happen. In my dream, the drive was the course I was on. As I was going, the dream was showing me a future encounter with someone who wants to be close to me, but their motive was wrong. The man in the dream appeared to have known me, however, I must add a but. The true spirit of this man was seen in operation, but I didn't understand his change in the dream. His characteristics were for my knowledge. Let me go to the next dream.

The next dream the Lord gave me was a tribe of people dancing in a circle. I heard the beat of what sounded like drums and loud chatting. Then the Lord showed me an older woman confronting me. She jumped in my face and moved back. The woman never said a word while she was doing this act. It made me feel like I was being taunted, like a bullying spirit. It was like this woman was provoking me. After being provoked, the Lord woke me up out of this dream. I now understood God showed me these things that were a reality which was hidden from me. These dreams were definitely trying to reveal a mystery to me. I just didn't know or understand their secret meanings.

Currently, back in my reality, I am still working. I am taking the time needed to spend time with God and focusing more on understanding my dreams. I am still legally married; however, we are living separately. I am trusting God and feel I will find the truth concerning everything in time. I must believe this until the truth is revealed. The unfaithfulness of my husband hasn't left me. I am still holding on to this, and I'm aware that I must leave from this place of hurt in my heart.

CHAPTER SIX

"PAINFUL SECRETS REVEALED"

Nowadays, I spend my time watching my children, making sure my home is secure, and my children are well supported. Since my husband is out of the house, our residence has become more manageable with less tension. The months are going by so fast. My oldest daughter and I are bonding, and things are good for now. I do hear more quarreling with my children though. I got news that my oldest daughter was talking to my husband through the kitchen window. This must have happened during the time I made an errand. I'm not sure. My sister took care of my children while I was working and when I had any errands, I informed her. Now that this has happened, I didn't want to take my focus off my oldest daughter knowing she talked with him. Then my oldest son spoke up and shared some news I hated hearing. I called my oldest daughter to inquire about her actions and what happened. My sister let her go upstairs to our apartment to get things from time to time. Remember, my sister lived downstairs. I was very upset about the communication my daughter had with my husband. I instructed my children that he didn't father, not to talk to him.

I asked her if she opened the door for him. She answered no, but I noticed my son getting irritated while we talked. I asked him why he was acting like this. These were his words, "Mom, she went to the door, and he got in the house. He took her in the bedroom. I heard her crying." I asked, "What was he doing to her?" Then my son replied, "I tried to stop him, and he grabbed my shirt and pushed me down. He kept hurting her. I couldn't stop him. He was on top of her and she was crying." That is what he told me. My oldest daughter was looking like a deer with their eyes caught in the headlights. I gathered my children together with a few of their clothes. I called my mom and asked her if she would look after them for me. I told her I had something to take care of and that I needed her help. My mom was more than glad to assist me. After I dropped my kids off with my mom, I returned home.

I called my husband and told him we needed to talk. I said it was important. It took about 30 minutes for him to arrive at my apartment. I heard him as he pulled into the driveway so I unlocked the door so he could come in. I didn't waste any time with chit chat.

I was angry with murder on my mind at this point. I am filled with rage. I declared to him, "I want you to know, I know everything. My son told me what you did to my daughter." He dropped his head. When he finally lifted his head, he looked at me exactly how my daughter looked after her brother told me what happened. He responded, "I don't know what happened. I didn't mean to hurt her." "You need help. What were you thinking? She is a baby for God's sake."

I had never been involved in a family matter of this sort. The one thing I knew was that I believed my son. I believed he heard my baby crying. He tried to protect his sister. He was just a child himself, but he tried. I know my son is telling the truth. My heart is questioning, "Why didn't she cry or show me a sign of my husband's wrongdoing?" My heart feels like it will burst right now. I didn't hear my baby crying. I let her down. I am her protector. I am supposed to know every detail of her life. I didn't hear her so I couldn't help her. Now many things are starting to make sense. I am recalling the incidents which are connected to this violation. I'm remembering some of my husband's actions. I honestly didn't exactly know what I should do so I called my Pastor. I needed Godly counsel and direction. I know we are taught that we are a new creature in Christ, and I believed I had to handle things differently. I know I had to seek counsel and guidance. I know I am saved and living a Christian life. We needed help! My daughter needed help! I needed help! I, with urgency, called my pastor. I didn't tell my pastor the details. He agreed to meet with us at the church.

My husband and I were sitting in my pastor's office. I came right out with it. I didn't know any other way to say it. I informed my pastor that my husband raped and molested my oldest daughter. My pastor, my covering, and my shepherd listened carefully. He appeared calm and focused as I expressed this horrible incident. After I ended talking, my pastor asked my husband with a straight face, "Is this true?" My husband was honest. He took accountability for his actions and answered my pastor, "I did it." There are so many stories of men lying about violating a child, but he admitted his wrongdoing. Although this was good on his part, I wasn't prepared for what happened next. My ears, my heart, and my soul couldn't imagine or conceive how my pastor would respond to my husband's admission of guilt. This is what my pastor said, "Why did you say you did it?" Then he told us about his family member who's in jail for the same thing. How he explained this story made it sound as if my daughter was not telling the truth. He told my husband he should not have said he did it. My pastor is telling my guilty husband how he should have never admitted his guilt. This was unbelievable! Not only did I not get help from my pastor, what he said was not Godly counsel. He didn't pray. He didn't give any verses from the bible on morality or sexual sins. He didn't rebuke my husband or correct him. He never brought up calling the police. He brought up his family member's situation which had nothing to do with my daughter's violation. This was devastating! I did not get any help from my pastor. He never even asked how my daughter was doing! I was crushed! When we left my pastor, I knew there was no other place to go but to the police. I believed my son's words and what he witnessed. I knew my daughter was not in any mental condition to help me help her. I didn't want to push her or press her too hard with questions. I didn't want her mental state to become any worse.

This situation was very taxing on my oldest daughter. Now that this secret was uncovered, I observed how my daughter was so withdrawn and isolated. I will never forget how she looked. Her appearance – her countenance – made my heart ache on a daily basis for my oldest daughter. She was afraid and totally dazed by her trauma. I was in shock myself with this painful information. So many times, I needed to take a deep breath to grab my thoughts. So many puzzle pieces were now coming together about certain things, and it was very overwhelming for me. My precious little princess is in a shattered place. I prayed for her daily and asked God to help her. We needed His intervention continuously.

The dream I had concerning my oldest daughter unfolded at a place with an urgency to roll the window up. I understand now that it was the kitchen window. The opened window was used by an evil person wanting to gain access to her. The dream was informing me that as I moved forward, one of my children needed help. This dream gave me absolute knowledge of coming danger, and the entry point. The dream was revealing a man wanted to gain particular access to my daughter. This was so overwhelming as I connected each dot and placed each puzzle piece together.

I got myself together and took my children to my sister's apartment downstairs. I drove to the police department. I didn't bring my daughter with me. I didn't want her to be more afraid. I went to the window to file a report and to get a warrant to have my husband arrested for raping and molesting my daughter. I feel afraid and alone. My heart is beating so hard, and I am so very angry. The officer I first talked with asked another officer to come take my complaint. I answered every question he asked me. I know it was God that kept me together during the questioning. After taking my complaint, the officer told me I was free to return home. I asked, "When will you pick him up for this crime?" The officer replied, "That's not the way this process is done. Another officer will come to your address and escort you to a facility. There your daughter will be given a physical by a certain doctor to determine if she was really raped." I couldn't believe my ears about this process. I wanted them to go and get my husband immediately. I went home and waited for the police.

When they came to take us to the facility, we were ready to go. So many things went through my mind. I was really concerned for my daughter. What exactly will they do while examining her? When we arrived at the Child Psychologists Office, surprisingly, it was not very far from home. They had me in a room looking through a two-way mirror. My daughter was in the other room just playing with dolls they provided for her. The child psychologist was there with her, and she talked kindly while observing her playing with the dolls. I watched through the two-way mirror. My daughter didn't do anything inappropriate while playing. I could not hear what my daughter was saying when she responded to the child psychologist. I thought she looked normal and didn't see anything wrong. The officer with me assured me we would be informed of what happens next. She sat on an activity rug for kids, and was offered more toys to play with. My daughter began to engage with the toys. To my knowledge, I saw nothing but her playing. The therapist was just talking with her as she handled the dolls and the other toys. I couldn't hear what my daughter was saying in response. I do know that she never looked up. She never moved from that one position as she played. Fifteen minutes passed by since she started playing with the toys. The therapist looked toward the two-way mirror and nodded her head up and down as to say yes. The police officer that was standing with me looked at me. This officer had already told me that the therapist would look at the mirror to let us know if my child was violated. This was the signal to the police and how the system works to bring criminal charges. I had to have specialist determination to have a legitimate case against my husband. The criminal psychologist is trained to know how to get the truth when no one else can. The officer got on his radio and said to his fellow officer, "Go pick him up for child rape." I wanted to get out of that room instantly. I wanted to run and grab my baby. How did this happen? I didn't hear my baby crying. Why did this happen to her? I am just unsettled with many, many thoughts as she was sitting on the floor playing and talking with the therapist. I am stuck. I can't move from this place in my mind. I waited for the officer and therapist to accompany my daughter back to me. The therapist instructed me that my little baby will need therapy. My thoughts were "How did this happen? How could a grown man do this to my baby?" I know my daughter is not a baby in terms of development. She is still my baby. She will always be my baby. The most dominant thought occurring is, "I didn't hear my baby crying." I was tormented imagining the act. How painful it must have been, and traumatic for her? I must be strong and not break down because of the pressure of this situation. I must get my daughter through this in a quiet healthy way. I don't know how to do this without the help of almighty God. I am determined to see her through this horrible situation. All I can think about is that this is my baby. I know I needed help as well because I was clueless about any of this. Even with my daughter playing with toys, right in front of me, I didn't see how she told the therapist what happened. I had no knowledge of how to recognize child rape. Lord help me.

The police had a warrant issued for the arrest of my husband. I also filed for divorce. The police didn't take long to locate and arrest

DR. APOSTLE ROBBIE CARSWELL

my husband. It took a total of almost two years to go through this process with the justice system. I arranged for therapy for my children. It was recommended and I agreed to it. The therapy went well, and I am very grateful. I don't know what I would have done without therapy, and the Lord. She helped me understand the healing process.

My husband is now in jail. I remember the day the officer came to my door. It was about 8:30 pm. I asked, "Who is it?" while I was coming to the door. The officer answered, "This is Officer Guilty." This is so ironic. I am in a child molestation case against my husband, and the officer who brought me the update name was, "Guilty." I was in disbelief concerning his name. I didn't trust anyone in my home, not even a police officer. I asked him for identification. He conveyed, "I am assigned to your case. I'm here to tell you that the offender has been arrested and charged with child rape and molestation. You will be notified of the upcoming court date." He left me with encouraging words and also added his reassurance that all would be well.

CHAPTER SEVEN

<u>"THE COURT TRIAL"</u>

The time has finally as I waited for this trial date for this crime against my baby. However, I don't want to sound as though all is well. My husband is in prison awaiting this trial for his actions. I stepped away from my job, remaining at home again, to protect my children and to assist my oldest daughter with the healing she so deeply needs. I was so depressed with everything pertaining to this situation. I had to pull myself up to be strength to my family.

Every day I woke up early to hear my daybreak CD with prayer and meditation. Morning by morning, I needed guidance and the help only the Lord could provide to show me the way. I asked Him daily to give me the wisdom to assist my oldest daughter and myself. I don't want to be in a marriage with a man that has an appetite for sex with young girls. I am angry because he betrayed our wedding vows. I am angry and hurt because I can't be angry with the person who has been in my bed with my husband. Now I know the truth. This other person is my baby girl. Do I have the right to be angry? Do I just let go of all judgment and focus only on my daughter's feelings? Oh God help me! I need you to keep my mind! I tried to keep my mind from wondering about the fact that the infidelity was with my daughter. My husband cheated on me by raping my daughter. I couldn't stop reflecting that she was only 8 years old. I know this may sound as if I am just rambling, but I can't think or focus on myself. My baby needs me. My daughter needs me. This chapter deals with all my questions and reflections of the days of not knowing, not understanding, and needing God's intervention. I wanted so bad to ask my daughter directly, "What happened with my husband?" "How did this happen?" I see my baby girl moving and playing. I know her innocence has been taken away from her. I want to know what is inside her mind. "How does she feel?" I want to know. I remember, during this time, asking God, "How do I deal with this in my family?" I am praying, but I don't hear anything from God. I cry, and I cry, because I didn't hear my baby crying. I am so very angry that I trusted a man! I am furious that he betrayed our marriage vows! I can't believe he violated my daughter! How could he do this to my child, or any child? I am faced with these questions. I think of myself as being a good mom and not a failure, but this situation and my guilt tells me, "Yes you are a failure, Robbie."

I sat in a chair at a Family Therapist office crying twice a week. My daughter received therapy as well. The therapist conveyed things I needed to do in the healing process for my family. With help from God and my therapist, I received closure from the hurt. My daughter needed extensive therapy. She is at the age of change in her life. I was there when she got her first period. I had to go to her school because she needed my presence. She was in the nurse's office when I arrived. We had a mother daughter conversation, and I took the time to explain everything concerning the change in her body. The nurse joined in our conversation. I think we made a good team teaching her the importance of hygiene care during this time in her life. Letting her know it will come every month around the same time. I informed her that she must tell me so I could provide the necessary personal items just in case she needs them, or if she's running out. I think she was doing a great job keeping herself aware of her cycle and her hygiene. However, I also had a rude awakening, like an epiphany, concerning my daughter. She could get pregnant. This was the hardest spiritual growth I ever had to walk through. I not only had to make sure influences and infatuations don't send her off, but I also knew now that she could very well get pregnant. Help me Jesus.

Because of this, I decided my daughter will not date or have a boyfriend until she turns 16.

In the meantime, I'm keeping her busy while the trial of her molestation case was in discovery. I have been forced to change my life for the rest of my life. I feel like I am walking through a bad dream. I say to myself in this hard place that I will wake up and everything will be back to normal. The next few weeks and months have been difficult. I only have a little strength, but God is my sustainer. I feel alone and unsure. (I have to get this chapter finished. The more I write the more things are being revealed.) The bible speaks of first natural then spiritual. I am trying to stabilize my family, and I want to scream, kick and fight. My emotions get carried away but the will to overcome is stronger than my present circumstance. We are going to get through this together in Jesus name.

CHAPTER EIGHT

"<u>FACE TO FACE</u>"

I am getting in the mental posture to face the man that molested and raped by daughter. The State's Attorney has informed me that it will be a bench trial. This type of trial has no jury. The judge will make the decision after hearing the case with the testimonies of my children. During this time of waiting, my children and I were focused on our physical and mental recovery. The Lord directed me to leave my local assembly, which is the church I was raised in. I joined a new worship assembly. It was best this way so my family would not be looked at or harassed. My husband was still a member of that assembly. I suppose he has a reason to stay since the pastor was on his side.

We are moving forward together. The court

date is here, and I am ready for justice for my daughter. After arriving at the courthouse, we were escorted to the judge's chambers. I was told I cannot be in the courtroom when my daughter takes the stand to testify. I am having some kind of emotional breakdown. I don't want her in the same room with that man! I sensed something evil taunting me. I discerned that my daughter would not be able to speak effectively, or freely, in front of the man who forcefully took control of her little body. How can I protect her if I'm not in the courtroom? She's been in therapy, and I followed the recommendations for her restoration and healing. I feel like I couldn't get her prepared to see her offender. This matter we are dealing with is spiritual. How can I teach her how to fight in the Spirit? How can I show her how to fight to have power over her mind? I am very uneasy and I'm learning the evil works of the devil. I know evil is real and this whole experience has been evil. How can I protect her now? Why can't I be in the courtroom? What type of action is keeping me from being in the courtroom? I wish I knew the reason why.

On the second day of the trial, the attorney for my children talked to me. She said, "Your daughter has become agitated and is not saying the same thing she stated on her first interview." I asked, "Was the offender in the courtroom while she spoke?" My children's attorney answered, "Yes, he was in the courtroom." I asked, "Can the judge, or could the judge, take her away in her chamber and allow her to speak to her alone?" I insisted and pleaded with my children's lawyer. I conveyed that the man is intimidating her. He has to be staring at her to cause her to be fearful. I know she was very challenged to tell on an adult. I understand our culture teaches that you don't tell what goes on in your home. However, I have taught her, no matter who it is, if a person makes her feel afraid to tell someone, tell someone anyway.

I know we believe our children have the courage to do whatever we, mom and/or dad, instilled in them. I am here to tell you that spiritual bondage and warfare is real. I know my daughter has a strong will. She spoke to her therapist very candidly about the rape she suffered by her stepfather. When an individual has been raped, it is more than just mental and physical. The spiritual aspect is just as critical. He had full control over my oldest daughter. I hated to admit this. He forced himself on her and the evil spirit inside of him, along with the words he said to her while he molested her, took her mind and will away from her. He broke her will and made it his own. He can just sit in the courtroom and look at her knowing she doesn't have it in her to testify against him. Now my daughter's attention, focus, and thoughts are everywhere but the courtroom. Her mind is totally shut down in his presence. I asked the attorney to tell my daughter to look at a clock or anything else but just don't look at him. I understood the spiritual transfer which took place during the rape now lives and abides inside of my daughter. When he came into the courtroom, my daughter was enslaved all over again. No matter how much they prepared her to testify against him, once she saw him, she was forced to submit to his will inside of her. Yes, his will has become her will because his evil spirit was dominating my daughter. When he put himself inside of my daughter, his spirit took possession of her mind, body, will, and soul.

The thought of my children having to relive and recreate the trauma of this situation in a courtroom is painful. The hurt, anger, and betrayal, all have become a horror movie for me. The attorney for my children explained the defense will call my oldest son to stand. I was confident my son would do well. He spoke up to me and I knew he could do the same on the stand. The defense attorney asked him, "Did you see your stepfather hurt your sister?" He responded, "Yes." The defense attorney asked my son, "How many times did he hurt her?"

He answered, "A whole lot of times. About 100 times." He also explained, "I knew he hurt her because I could hear her crying every time he would leave the bedroom. After a little while, she would stop crying and go to sleep." There were no further questions for my son. He told the truth. It was very hard to hear my daughter was violated so many times. My son heard his sister, but I didn't hear my baby crying. My heart hurts in such a deep way that I can't describe it, but I'm satisfied my son gave his testimony. He wasn't intimidated. Thank you, Lord. As I thought about it, which I couldn't help but think about it, I believe this happened while I worked overnight. My baby was easy prey for him knowing I was working. I trusted him. I loved this man and married him. How could he do such a thing? I didn't notice any trauma in my oldest daughter. I'll say this another way: I didn't see any change in my oldest daughter by the trauma she experienced. She was the same little girl in front of me. This made me desire to never work again overnight. I can't imagine her experience. Now she's next to take the stand for the defense. I hope my discernment is wrong concerning her.

The conclusion rests with the testimony of my daughter. The defense asked her one question. "How many times did your stepfather rape you?" After being asked this question, she immediately locked eyes on the man that raped and molested her. She whispered, "Only one time." while she looked at him in the courtroom. She appeared to be in a daze. I was informed by my son and by my children's attorney. She looked very confused by him looking at her. I knew he was projecting his spirit at her causing her to fear. Well..., it worked. The defense rested, no other witnesses were called, and the testimonies were now closed.

I was brought out of the judge's chamber to hear the closing remarks from the judge. It was a long, drawn-out trial. The total time was about one month back and forth. My husband, ex-husband, was in prison for about two years waiting for this trial. I am anticipating a guilty verdict. Here's what happened. The judge asked me to hear her clearly. She declared, "Based on the testimony of the two children. I can only rule for the defense. The two testimonies created reasonable doubt." The judge looked at my ex-husband and told him these words. "I don't think you are innocent. However, because this is a bench trial, I cannot rule for the children." She looked at me and declared, "He will not ever be innocent." She encouraged me to continue the good I have begun with my children. The judge assured me that she had to release him. I can sense many will say he got off. I want you to know that because of spiritual warfare my daughter was not justified in the court system. I believe God is yet in control. I gathered myself and my things, and proceeded out of the courtroom. I focused on getting us home. Because the trial was over, I had a spirit of relief for my children. We can move on from this place in our lives. I am disappointed, nevertheless, I understand what happened. I know for a fact, if my ex-husband was not allowed in the courtroom while my daughter was on the witness stand, she would have stood in liberty without fear or mind control. The thing which I feared the most has happened to us. How could the judge allow children to be in the same room as the predator they must testify against? Don't they know the predator will use intimidation tactics? I felt it was inhumane and cruel. The law is for the lawless. Knowing what I know today, why wasn't my former pastor called to testify? The predator admitted he did it to him in front of me. Whether it was one time or one hundred times, he raped my daughter. How is this reasonable doubt? There may be doubt about the number of times, but he still did it. I will never understand the uncertainty of a bench trial. I will, however, teach women who are dealing with this same situation or who are experiencing this in some capacity, to seek spiritual guidance. I would encourage counsel in spiritual warfare to cover the mind of your children. This will be another book at a later time.

CHAPTER NINE

<u>"THE AFTERMATH"</u>

I didn't hear my baby crying taunted my very soul. I could not escape trying to understand how a man who was supposed to be a role model in our home, is known to me as a child predator. After the trial, we remained in the same apartment. Our location was very convenient near their school. After all the settling which has gone on since the trial, I am yet careful. I know in my heart with sincere understanding; nothing will ever be the same. The dynamic of my family has shifted forever. We are moving forward together in love and unity embracing each other with each step we take. I feel as though an evil has been loosed in the earth and it's searching for my daughter. I will never be at ease when it comes to their safety again. I can't keep them inside our house forever. Children want to go outside to play and see their friends. My oldest daughter is interested in after school curriculums. I am afraid, but I must allow her to grow up and have a normal life.

I thought it was a great new beginning. She was involved with the Junior Beta Club. I allowed her to attend those meetings, in the morning, before her school started. She was excited about it and was fully active to my knowledge. My oldest son can now lead his younger sister and brother to school since his big sister was now in a club. He walked her halfway to school each day she had club meetings. He was giving her a little help and security, which also gave me some peace. I reminded them, if they saw their former stepfather, do not talk to him and go a different route away from him. I thought nothing else could go wrong. You figure no one would try to violate or contact a minor as a sexual predator again, right?

The weeks have turned into months. They have passed by so quickly since she joined the Junior Beta Club. I noticed her faithfulness to the club, and I was happy she found something she loved doing. One day I had an appointment, and my children had to attend it with me. On this day, she had a meeting prior to my appointment. My son walked her halfway to school that morning, and when I knew the meeting had ended, I had him go back to their school to escort his sister home. He went to their school and returned home informing me that their school was closed. I thought to myself, "It can't be closed." In my mind, I thought my daughter was in a Junior Beta Club meeting. He also told me the janitor saw him at the door and asked, "Why are you here so early? No one is here yet." This caused me to call their school to speak with the attendance office. The information I received was very disturbing and alarming. It was expressed to me that there was no club meeting that morning, so the doors of the school were locked. I was furious!!! Why would my daughter lie, and where did she go for an hour before school? Was she secretly hanging out with her friends? Did she have a boyfriend she didn't want me to find out about? Where did she go? My mind was racing with different reasons why she lied to me. At the time I talked with the attendance office, their school was open, and students were in their classes. They checked their attendance list and my daughter was present. This was good to hear, but she had a lot of explaining to do. Maybe she forgot there was no meeting today and went to the park instead of coming back home. I needed answers! I asked the school to give my daughter a message. They took my message and had my daughter come down for an early release at the time I requested. When I picked her up from school, I had my other children in our car. I consciously had to keep myself together during the ride. I didn't want to question her in front of her siblings, and I needed to be well composed during the appointment. I waited to question her once we returned home.

I called my daughter to the living room with

I DIDN'T HEAR MY BABY CRYING

an authoritative tone. I asked her directly, "Where were you today!?" I confronted her with the evidence the school gave me and boldly told her she didn't have a Junior Beta Club meeting. I wasn't prepared for her answer. She started crying, and what she said hurt my ears, and crushed my heart. She answered me saying my ex-husband had been following her to school and he forced her into his car. The next chain of events was terrifying. She told me he took her to his mother's apartment and raped her again. He told her he would hurt her if she told on him. This caused her to be afraid and very scared. He was raping and molesting my baby again. My heart fell to the floor within me. My pulse raced loudly as I called the police in my town. The police told me because it happened in the next town, to go to the police station there and file a complaint. My daughter was more compliant with the police than she was the first time before the trial. She told the police where he took her and described everything she saw in his mom's apartment. She gave them accurate detailed information. The police went to his mom's address on record. The things my daughter saw were recognized by the police. I was told to have the case reopened against my ex. This became very overwhelming naturally and spiritually. The stress and pressure has become so challenging and practically unbearable. How can a man spend time in prison, then be released, and come out to the same vile crime!? My mind…, oh my God my mind! He got off! Now he's raping my daughter again! I can't keep him from my daughter. I can't watch her

24 hours a day. I know a spirit is trying to destroy my daughter. I don't want to lose my daughter to the state again. I know that her soul must be crying out for help. Why didn't she tell me when this first happened? What is going on? How is this happening again? I now understand there is a spirit that has overtaken my baby. My ex still owns her will although she's been in therapy. At least she told the police details which did implicate him. I am living in a spiritual war zone. My ex-husband can access her at will. This knowledge shakes my soul. I am told there is nothing that can be done. I had to build another case and as they say, "Catch him in the act." I filed a restraining order against my ex-husband. I must get my daughter totally away from him! I made a decision to send her out of the state. I reached

out to her biological father. I asked for his help and told him what our daughter has been through. He was upset, yet very willing to help her. The pressure and fear of him raping my daughter again was forcing me to make this drastic decision. The police were saying he had already served his time for the crime. How did he serve time for a crime when he was released from prison? Even though the judge knew he was guilty, the judge still let him go because of reasonable doubt. The time he served was for nothing now that he's back to raping my daughter. I'm trying to get the police to see he was stalking her. He was in contact with her unlawfully. Doesn't this mean anything? He forced her into his car and raped her again. This is a new crime against my daughter. My mind was very distraught, and I could only imagine what was going on inside my oldest daughter's mind. She didn't tell me the first time and now she didn't tell me this time. Why didn't she tell me? I started making excuses for her. She was so afraid of him that she willfully submits to rape. She had no strength to run away. No strength to speak about it until I confronted her. I'm glad I had an appointment that day or I may have never found out. She always looked the same around me. She didn't show any signs she was being molested. These thoughts helped me decide to relocate her, out of the state, to be with her father. She will live far away from this evil predator. He will never find her again. This made the most sense to me with our law enforcement doing nothing. I needed peace of mind concerning my baby and I believed living with her father was the answer. The answer to keeping my daughter safe from this evil man, protected by her father, and we can all have peace of mind. Her father and I talked about everything. I wished I would have told him sooner. Maybe this wouldn't have happened a second time. Maybe this decision would have been made sooner to live with her father.

CHAPTER TEN

"THE POWER OF LOVE"

I have now come to a reasonable place of peace. My daughter has relocated to Las Vegas to live with her father. I am really going through in my mind presently. I know that she is safe. I believe this in my heart. I thank God for watching over her all these months. I talked with her on the phone weekly. She had a regular schedule with her dad. I hear happiness and liberty in her voice as she was getting settled in Las Vegas. I have come to realize only God has the answer to everything from this point. I have been asking God to guide me and to keep my heart and mind. I don't want to be away from my daughter, but I have to live with this decision. I miss her so much, but in my heart of hearts, I know this is the right decision for her young life. I'm so happy my ex-husband can't find her anymore. He can't use his demonic influence or his filthy desire over her anymore. I am enjoying my other children, but my mind is on my daughter night and day. I have to trust my decision and be at peace with it. There's only one thing on my mind, Lord protect her and help her finish school on time. I keep asking God, "How long will she live there?" I suppose she will be there until it's safe for her to return home. I suppose she's at home now. Her new home. This thought really gave me peace. She's in an environment without traumatic memories. Help her adjust to her new home Lord.

This was the most painful time of my daughter's life. I don't think of myself as often because I'm constantly thinking of her. I asked

God to allow me to see her in the Spirit. The time that has transpired has taught me to pray strategically. The power of God's will in prayer is leading me to deeper realms in the Spirit. My prayer and intercession, with the reading of my Word, has increased. I am currently asking the Lord to reveal the life of baby. I know she is not an infant, but she will always be my baby.

She has been living out of state for a few months now. I am still asking God to help me discern my daughter in the Spirit and I'm also asking Him, "Is it well?" We are still having our phone conversations every week, and I also have talks with her dad. Her father has been taking great care of her. I'm seeing how much she loves him, and I'm also seeing she's good for him. Her healing is taking place. This is working out better than I had hoped. Thank you Jesus.

I am grateful the Holy Spirit is increasing my prayer time and my capacity to learn in the Spirit. I want to know with assurance that my daughter is alright. I fast and pray for an answer from the Lord. While I went through this situation, I never lost my praise or stopped attending my church. I was faithful to God, but I can't say I didn't feel broken, undone, and a failure. I never stopped seeking healing for myself. I had to fight the agonizing thoughts of not knowing what was happening to my daughter. I had many tears because I didn't hear my baby crying. I could always tell what was wrong when I heard my children cry. In this situation the enemy was trying to take my prayer focus. I had to pull on strength in the

Spirit to keep me. I know God will bring me through this. I believe every mother has gone through a panic when their children are away from home. The torment in my mind and heart was causing my imagination to run wild. I am asking the Lord to let me see that she is ok. Lord just let me see her. I know I heard her voice every week and her father kept saying she was in good hands, but I needed something more than this. I needed God to do something special for my perfect peace of mind. I want to encourage every reader of my book. I am here to tell you that God does answer prayer.

I remained consistent in prayer and fasting for God to show me my daughter in the Spirit. I cannot tell you the day or the time, but I can tell you the Lord gave me a vision of my daughter. I saw my daughter on the campus of a school. There was a crowd of students surrounding her. I feel my heart beating so hard as I tell you this vision. I saw a girl confronting my daughter. I discerned my daughter was afraid of this girl. The girl hit my daughter in the face causing her to fall down and cry. I cried out to God, "Let my baby hear my voice!" In the Spirit I cried out to her, "Get up baby and fight!" She looked around as if she was looking for me, and pulled herself up. I saw my daughter stand up for herself and begin to swing back saying, "Don't put your hands on me anymore!" The vision happened at the right appointed time in my life. I could hear my baby crying. We now had a connection between us. We were connected by the Lord in the Spirit. I started crying and thanking God for comforting my heart. I discerned my daughter and could see her continually from this point onward. The agony of a violation in the family can make a parent feel like they are nothing. You can feel so broken, I know I did, and that defeat is all the parents can understand. As I sought the Lord, God showed me that I had a gift given by Him. Life can throw punches that we don't see. When God let me see my daughter in the vision, I was made whole. The vision was also confirmation that it was time for her to come home. "I didn't hear my baby crying" is a moment in time. It was not a lack in my ability as a mother; however, I didn't have the skills to recognize trauma in my children. Nor did I know how to recognize a child predator. I thanked God for sharpening my discernment and revealing the truth. I walk in greater grace since all this pain occurred. I am stronger and wiser now.

This is the closure of a time in my life, and my daughter's life. I made arrangements for her to return home. As I embraced my daughter, I thanked God for her life, health, and strength. We didn't talk about anything about the past. We allowed the healing to continue and embrace every new day together. I could not have made it without great spiritual parents. The Lord blessed my family with a real spiritual covering. My Pastor Jinks A. Arnold, and leading Lady Donna Arnold. They took us under their care and nurtured my family back to health. The torment of not hearing my baby crying was the symptom of being without discernment, natural or spiritual. One day I asked my daughter a question. The question was concerning the vision I just shared with you in this book. She answered, "Momma, I did have a fight at school." I then asked, "What happened during the fight?" She confirmed everything that God had given me in my vision. My soul became free to talk, and I began telling my daughter that everything that happened was not her fault. I shared how much I loved her, and nothing would ever stop me from loving her. I explained how sorry I was that my ex-husband molested her. It felt so good to apologize to my baby. Dealing with this traumatic experience has taught me many things. I've learned so much. I thank God for teaching me how to stand. My children are gifts, and they are very precious to me. We've overcome so much together, and I give God the praise for it.

Thanks for reading my story and thank you for your support. God bless you.

I must obey God, by releasing this prayer. "Father, I come to you, and I pray for every woman reading this book. I ask you Lord God to let your healing virtue touch every area in their lives. Father, I ask you to bring forgiveness into each and every woman that has been raped or molested. You said if we don't forgive, our Heavenly Father will not forgive us. The people that have violated our loved ones, have mercy on them. Lord save and deliver them from generational curses and ungodly soul ties. Lord God, I ask you to give them a heart of repentance. Father, I ask you to break and destroy the yoke. Save them Lord from the evil that is inside of them. Lord, let the healing begin fresh with no setbacks or drawbacks in the name of Jesus. The bible reads in the book of Psalm 90:12, "Teach us to number our days that we may apply our hearts unto wisdom." We are moving forward and thanking you Lord for your grace and mercies. Give us wisdom to love unconditionally and let us continue to be hearers and doers of your Word. In Jesus name. Amen. God bless you and keep you always is my prayer.

I

Didn't

HEAR

My Baby

CRYING

DR. APOSTLE ROBBIE CARSWELL

I

Didn't

HEAR

My Baby

CRYING

DR. APOSTLE ROBBIE CARSWELL

UNFAZED PUBLISHING
YOUR MIND IS OUR BUSINESS

TAMPA FLORIDA

www.UnfazedPublishing.com

PRECISION IN AUTHOR THOUGHT

YOUR MIND IS OUR BUSINESS

www.ingramcontent.com/pod-product-compliance
Lightning Source LLC
LaVergne TN
LVHW021346080426
835508LV00020B/2139